The Mommy Journal

The Mommy Journal

Letters to Your Child

by Tracy Broy

Andrews McMeel
Publishing

Kansas City

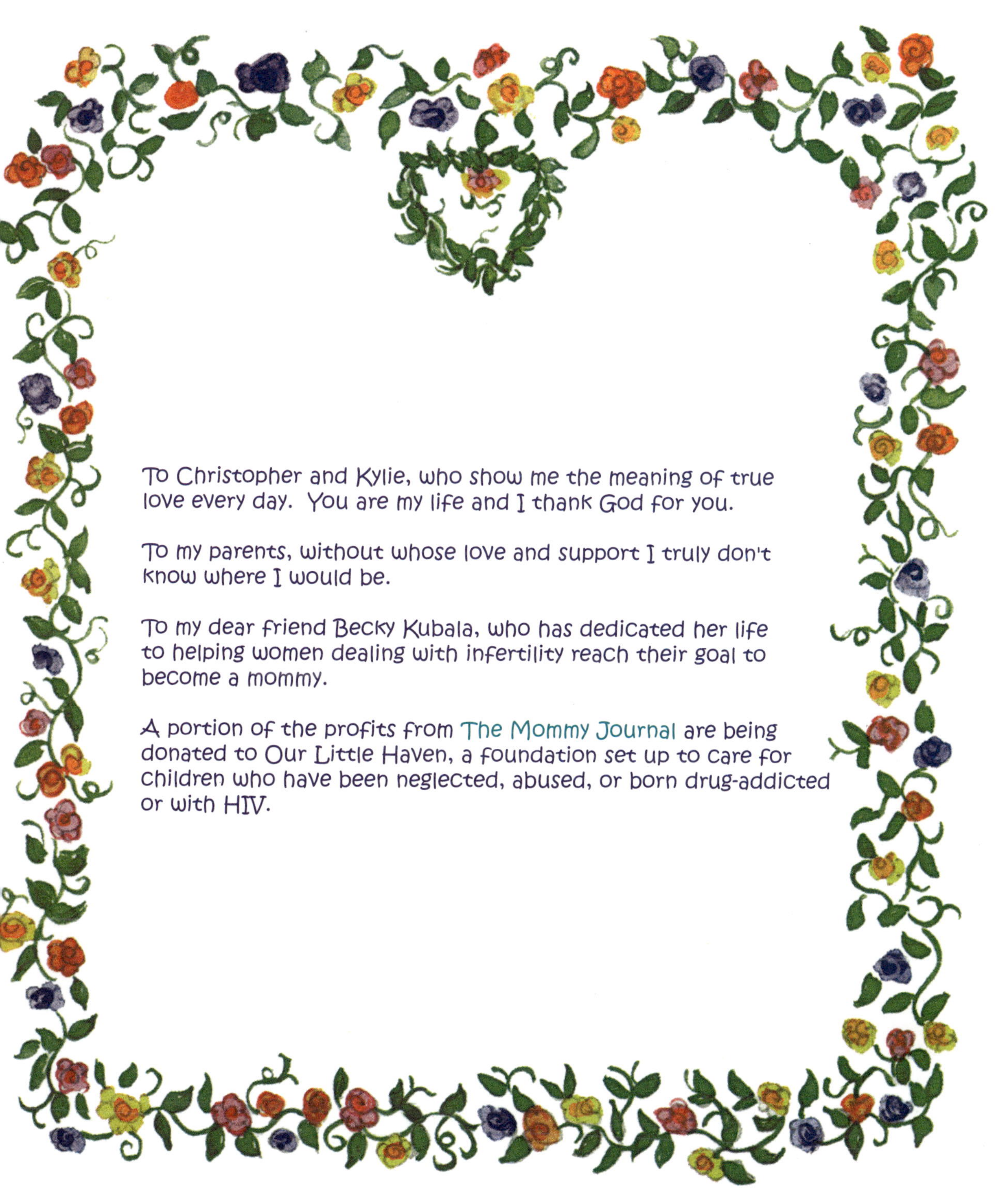

To Christopher and Kylie, who show me the meaning of true love every day. You are my life and I thank God for you.

To my parents, without whose love and support I truly don't know where I would be.

To my dear friend Becky Kubala, who has dedicated her life to helping women dealing with infertility reach their goal to become a mommy.

A portion of the profits from The Mommy Journal are being donated to Our Little Haven, a foundation set up to care for children who have been neglected, abused, or born drug-addicted or with HIV.

Dear Mommies,

I truly believe that the best thing I have ever done and ever will do is become a mom. The reason I created The Mommy Journal is because I wanted to share with moms a way to create and capture the memories of their children's lives. Let me explain.

When I was seven months pregnant I was sitting in the finished nursery rocking my unborn children and reading them a story. The twins began to kick each other and this overwhelming feeling of love rushed over me. I decided to write them a letter to capture my feelings and be able to look back on this special time in my life. I wanted to remember exactly how I was feeling. I sealed the letter and decided that I would give Christopher and Kylie this letter when they were older and could understand and have some insight into my feelings. I wrote another letter to them on the night they were born and have since written them a letter each night before their birthday.

When the twins were about six months old, my son was making this funny sound when he was getting ready to go to sleep. I remember thinking how cute it was and my mother said, "You think you will remember this, but you won't." I realized how true that was and decided to keep a journal of the things my childen do and say. I don't journal every day because there are days (believe it or not) that are pretty uneventful. For the most part, however, I have plenty to write about.

I plan to give Christopher and Kylie these letters when they are adults and can truly appreciate them. I will be giving them a letter for each year of their childhood and hopefully give them a tradition they can pass down to their children. I feel I am giving them a part of myself, so that even when I am not around, they will always have a part of me with them.

Here's how to journal in your Mommy Journal. After you put the kids down, make yourself a hot cup of tea, relax in your favorite writing place, and think about what happened that day. Write down the funny things that were said or done, or maybe you had a trying day and you need to get your frustrations out. Please don't feel the pressure to journal every day. Life is sometimes overwhelming. Write when you can; it only has to take five minutes.

On the night before your child's birthday, go back through the journal and write a letter to your child based on what you've written in the past year. Seal it, put in your Keepsake Box, and get ready to capture the next year.

Happy journaling!

Tracy

P.S. I have included in the journal activities and songs that Christopher, Kylie, and I enjoy. I know there are days when I'm at a loss for something to do with them, so I thought I would share our favorites.

Date:

Date:

Date:

Date: _______

Date: _______

Date: _______

Date:

Date:

Date:

Date:———————

Date:———————

Date:———————

Date: ———————

Date: ———————

Date: ———————

Date:————————

Date:————————

Date: ———————

Date: ———————

Date: ———————

Date:

Date:

Date:

Date:————————

Date:————————

Date:————————

Date:——————————

Date:——————————

Date:——————————

Date:————————

Date:————————

Date:————————

Date: ___________

Date: ___________

Date: ___________

Date:—————————

Date:—————————

Date:

Take a picture of your newborn
on the same day of each month
for her first year. You will be
amazed at the changes a
month can make.

Date:

Date:

Date:—————

Date:—————

Date:—————

Date: ______________

Date: ______________

Date: ______________

Date:

Date:

Date:

Date: ——————————

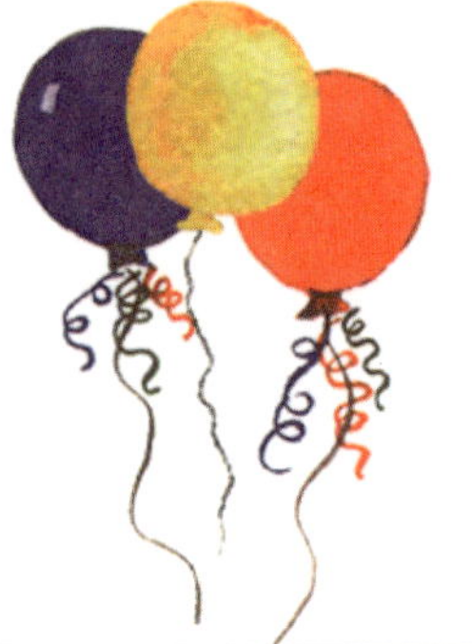

Date: ——————

Date: ——————

The Purple Cat Song

Out of the blue, riding in the car one day, my daughter Kylie started singing this song. She starts it off every time with a purple cat. It's a great song to sing while in the car because you can substitute what your children see outside. Here's how it goes:

Purple Cat, Purple Cat,

What do you see?

I see a car

Looking at me.

Car, Car

What do you see?

I see a school bus

Looking at me.

School Bus, School Bus

What do you see?

I see an airplane

Looking at me.

And so on, and so on . . .

Date: _______________

Date: _______________

Date: _______________

Encourage your children to
dream. They will become
what you expect of them. If
your expectations are high,
what they expect of themselves
will be high as well.

Date:____________

Date:____________

Date:____________

Date: ___________

Date: ___________

Date: ___________

Date:____________

Date:____________

Date:____________

Date: ____________________

Date: ____________________

Date: ____________________

Date:————————

Date:————————

Date:————————

Date: ___________

Date: ___________

Date: _______

Date: _______

Date: _______

Date: ___________

Date: ___________

Date: ___________

Date:

Date:

Date:

Date: ___________

Date: ___________

Date: ___________

Date:______________

Date:______________

Date:______________

Date: —————

Date: —————

Date: —————

Date:______

Date:______

Date:______________

Date:______________

Date:______________

Date: ——————

Date: ——————

Date: ——————

Date:———————

Date:———————

Date:———————

Date: ___________

Date: ___________

Date: ___________

Date: ______

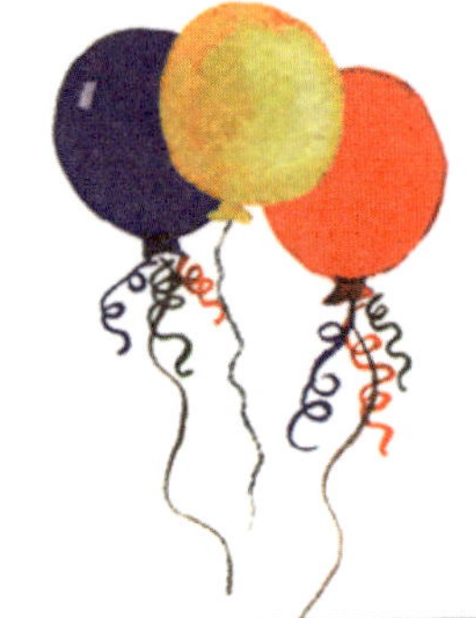

Date: ______

Date: ______

Mr. Alligator

Thanks to Mrs. Sinnett for teaching us this song.

Words:	Actions:
Five little monkeys	Swing your hand back
swinging from a tree,	and forth (five fingers up)
Teasing Mr. Alligator,	
You can't catch me,	Point finger while shaking
No, you can't catch me	your head.
Along came Mr. Alligator	Put hands together and
Hungry as can be,	move them in a zigzag
And he snapped that	motion as an alligator
monkey right out of	would while swimming.
that tree.	Clap hands to make a
	snapping sound.

Following verses:

Four little monkeys . . .

Three little monkeys . . .

Two little monkeys . . .

One little monkey . . .

Date: ________________

Date: ________________

Date: ________________

Date: —————

Date: —————

Date: —————

Date: ———————

Date: ———————

Date: ———————

Date: _________

Date: _________

Date: _________

Date: ______________

Date: ______________

Date: ______________

Date:____________

Date:____________

Date:____________

Date:————————

Date:————————

Date: ________________

Date: ________________

Date: ________________

Date: ______________

Date: ______________

Date: ______________

Date: ________

Date: ________

Date: ________

Date: ______________

Date: ______________

Date: ______________

Date: ___________

Date: ___________

Date: ___________

Date:—————————

Date:—————————

Date:—————————

Date:

Date:

Date:______

Date:______

Date:______

Date: ——————————

Date: ——————————

Date: ——————————

Date: —————————

Date: —————————

Date: —————————

Date: ______________

Date: ______________

Date: ______________

Date:————————

Date:————————

Date:————————

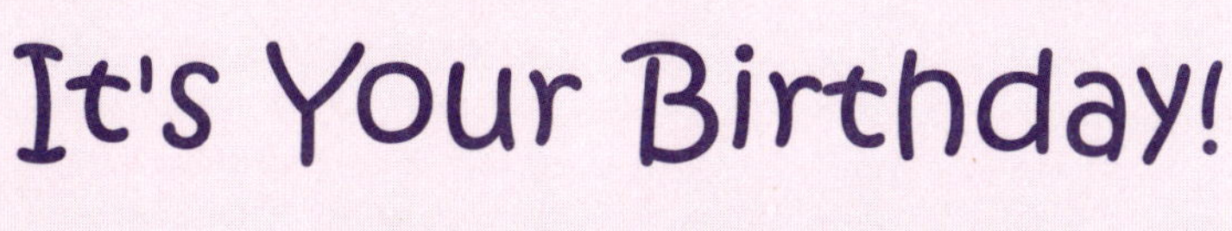

It's Your Birthday!

We all want to make our child's birthday as special as we can, so here are a few suggestions:

- Choose a book or books from this list and begin to read it the week before your child's birthday:

  Happy Birthday, by Gail Gibbons

  Benjamin's 365 Birthdays, by Judi Barrett

  The Secret Birthday Message, by Eric Carle

  Today Is Your Birthday, by P. K. Hallinan

- Have a plate that says "It's Your Special Day" and use it for everyone in the family on their birthday. We made ours at a local ceramic shop.

- Let your children bake and decorate a cake for themselves. When they are finished, let them eat it however they want!

- One month before your child's birthday, start a countdown on the calendar. Talk about what a birthday is and tell them the story about the day they were born.

Date: ___________

Date: ___________

Date: ___________

Date: ______

Date: ______

Date: ______

Date: ______________

Plant a garden with your children. It doesn't have to be very big. They will learn about different kinds of vegetables and flowers and how they grow. You may even get them to eat a vegetable or two!

Date: ______________

Date: ______________

Date: _______

Date: _______

Date: _______

Date: _______________

Date: _______________

Date: _______________

Date: ________

Date: ________

Date: ________

Date:———————

Date:———————

Date:

Date:

Date:

Date: _______________

Date: _______________

Date: _______________

Date: ———————

Date: ———————

Date: ———————

Date: _____________

Bake cookies with your children and give them to residents in a local nursing home. Children love to feel productive and cooking is a great way for them to create something. This also gives you a chance to instill in them the joy of giving to others.

Date: _____________

Date: _____________

Date: ___________

Date: ___________

Date: ___________

Date: _______________

Date: _______________

Date: _______________

Date:————————

Date:————

Date: ___________

Date: ___________

Date: ___________

Date:____________

Date:____________

Date:____________

Date: ___________________

Date: ___________________

Date: ___________________

Date: __________

Date: __________

Date: __________

Date: ——————

Date: ——————

Date: ——————

Homemade Play Clay

You can always buy Play-Doh at the store, but it's more fun to make. Keep several colors ready to play with on rainy days. For warm, sunny days, set up a child-size table and chairs under a shade tree and let the kids have their fun outside.

2 cups flour	2 TBSP. oil
1 cup salt	1 TSP. food coloring
1 TSP. cream of tartar	2 cups water

Mix ingredients together in a heavy saucepan and heat over medium heat, stirring constantly until dough leaves sides of the pan. Let it cool completely then knead out any bubbles. Store in plastic bags.

Date: ______________

Date: ______________

Date: ______________

Date: __________

Date: __________

Date: __________

Date: _______________

Date: _______________

Date: _______________

Date: ______________

Date: ______________

Date: ______________

Date: ______________

Date: ______________

Date: ______________

Date: ______________

Date: ______________

Date: ______________

Date: ———————

Date: ———————

Date: ____________

Date: ____________

Date: ____________

Date: ______________________

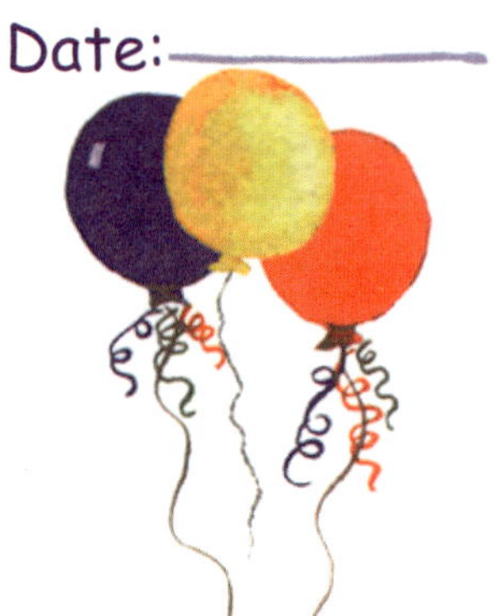

Date: ______________________

Date: ______________________

Date: ___________

Date: ___________

Date: ___________

Date:

Date:

Date:

Date: ——————

Date: ——————

Date: ——————

Date: ——————

Date: ——————

Date: ——————

Date:——————————

Date:——————————

Date: ____________

Go to a ceramic shop and imprint your child's handprint on a mug or plate with her age underneath it. This makes a great gift or keepsake. While you are there, let her paint something on her own. She will feel a great sense of accomplishment.

Date: ____________

Date: ____________

Date: ______________

Date: ______________

Date: ______________

Date: ―――――――――

―――――――――――――――――――――――――――――――――――

Date: ―――――――――

―――――――――――――――――――――――――――――――――――

Date: ―――――――――

Date: ———————

Date: ———————

Date: ———————

Date: ________

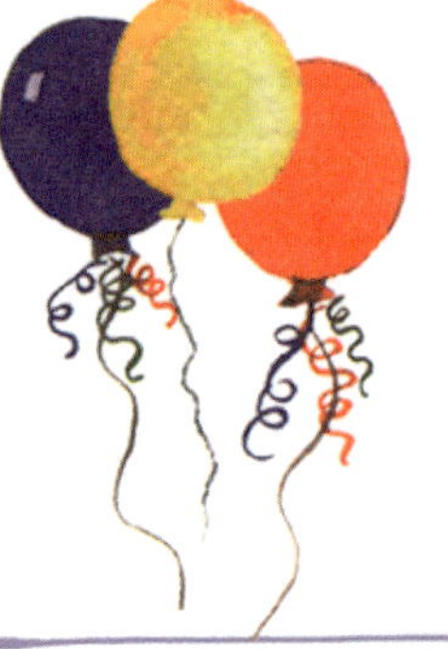

Date: ________

Date: ________

Let's Read Together

Here are some suggestions of books for you and your children to read together. Make storytime fun! On the weekends, we pop popcorn and for an hour or two before bedtime, we have a little reading party. These are some of our favorites:

Chicka Chicka Boom Boom, by Bill Martin Jr. and John Archambault
All by Myself, by Mercer Mayer
Goodnight Moon, by Margaret Wise Brown
Love You Forever, by Robert Munsch
Guess How Much I Love You, by Sam McBratney
Chicken Soup with Rice, by Maurice Sendak
Bye Bye Baby, by Janet Ahlberg
Twinkle, Twinkle Little Bug, by Katharine Ross
The Mitten, by Jan Brett
I Can! Can You?, by Peggy Parrish
On the Day You Were Born, by Debra Frasier
Little Bear (series of books), by Maurice Sendak
The Very Hungry Caterpillar, by Eric Carle
So Much, by Trish Cooke
Owl Babies, by Martin Waddell
Commotion in the Ocean, by Giles Andreae
Do You Want to Be My Friend?, by Eric Carle
Corduroy, by Don Freeman
Deep in the Forest, by Brinton Turkle
Cloudy with a Chance of Meatballs, by Judi Barrett
Mr. Rabbit and the Lovely Present, by Charlotte Zolotow
Anthony the Perfect Monster, by Angelo DeCesare
I Like Me, by Nancy Carlson
We are All Alike . . . We are All Different, by the Cheltenham
    Elementary School Kindergartners
Read-Aloud Rhymes for the Very Young, by Jack Prelutsky

Date: —————

Date: —————

Date: —————

Date:

Date:

Date:

Date: ________________

Date: ________________

Date: ________________

Date:

Date:

Date:

Date: ___________

Date: ___________

Date: ___________

Date: ______

Date: ______

Date: ______

Date: ———————

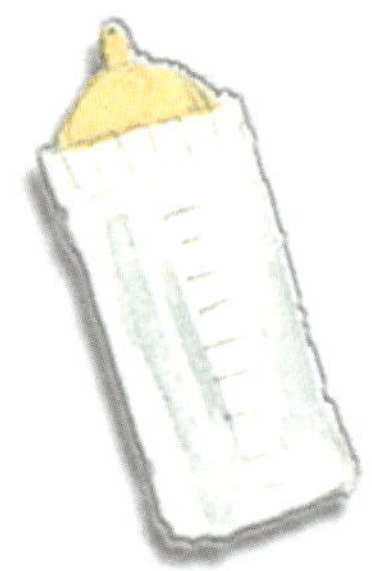

Date: ———————

Date:__________

Date:__________

Date:__________

Date: ——————

Date: ——————

Date: ——————

Date: _______________

Date: _______________

Date: _______________

Date: ——————

Date: ——————

Date: ——————

Date:____________

Date:____________

Date:____________

Date: _______

Date: _______

Date: _______

Date: 

Date:

Date: —————

Date: —————

Date: —————

Date:

Date:

Date:

Date:————————

Date:————————

Date:————————

Date: ______

Date: ______

Date: ______

Date: ______________

Date: __________

Date: __________

Explore, Explore, Explore

On a pretty summer day when bugs are all around, go for an adventure into the woods. Pack a lunch, take a blanket, and be explorers. Here are a few things you might want to take along:

A bug box for storing the little varmints you catch

Tweezers for picking up those slimy creatures

Bug spray, so you don't come home with any itchies

A bug net

A magnifying glass

Towelettes

A camera

Food (for you, not the bugs!)

Plenty to drink

Around Your Town . . .

Investigate all of the museums in your area and nearby places for your kids to go. You can call your local tourism bureau and have them send you information. It's fun to see what your city or town has to offer for your children to explore.

Have fun!

Date: ——————

Date: ——————

Date: ——————